Healing the Soul *of a* Woman

STUDY GUIDE

Healing
the Soul
of a
Woman

STUDY GUIDE

JOYCE MEYER

NEW YORK   NASHVILLE

FaithWords

Hachette Book Group

1290 Avenue of the Americas, New York, NY 10104

faithwords.com

twitter.com/faithwords

First Edition: September 2018

FaithWords is a division of Hachette Book Group, Inc. The FaithWords name and logo are trademarks of Hachette Book Group, Inc.

The publisher is not responsible for websites (or their content) that are not owned by the publisher.

The Hachette Speakers Bureau provides a wide range of authors for speaking events. To find out more, go to www.hachettespeakersbureau.com or call (866) 376-6591.

ISBN: 978-1-5460-1178-1

Printed in the United States of America

LSC-C

10 9 8 7 6 5 4 3 2

CONTENTS

INTRODUCTION

Can a woman who has been hurt deeply either by circumstances in her life or by a person she loved and trusted be healed? Can her heart and soul be healed? Can she love and trust once again? As a woman who was sexually abused by my father, abandoned by my mother, and cheated on by my first husband, I can say without hesitation, "Yes!" If you are living with a wounded soul and feeling alone, unloved, and misunderstood, I can promise you that you do not have to stay that way.

Your soul is the inner part of you, and it is a very important part. When we have wounded souls, we do not enjoy life, and that goes against what Jesus offers us in John 10:10 (read it now if you don't know this Scripture).

I'm pretty open about my testimony of being abused and how God helped me to heal. You can read some of it in the introduction of *Healing the Soul of a Woman*, and you'll discover more of it as you continue to read the book and work through this study guide. Whether you, too, have been abused by someone or you suffer from other wounds in your soul, I want you to know that God wants to heal you everywhere you hurt.

As you work through the questions and activities in this book, I pray you will discover the beautiful gift of healing God wants to give to each of us, His beloved. By reading each chapter in *Healing the Soul of a Woman* before you begin to work on the corresponding chapter in this book, you will have the opportunity to contemplate areas you need God's healing in and how to activate them in your life.

Each chapter in this study guide contains some or all of these four parts:

- **In Touch with Yourself** starts off each chapter, helping you to reflect on and ponder the main ideas in the chapter. It sets the stage for you to dive deeper and prepare for healing.
- **Explore God's Word** gives you Scriptures from the chapter and other Scriptures with the same theme to show you what God's Word says about each subject. You may want to make it a point to memorize any Scripture that really speaks to you—or says something you know you need to carry with you. Consider writing those Scriptures on small cards or using sticky notes on your phone or computer to help you remember them.
- **Healing in Action** requires you to do something. I don't want you to just read the healing words and not apply them. For each chapter, I give you a specific assignment to promote your healing. Check this section frequently and make notes of your progress.
- **Remember** (chapters 7-23 only) includes the main takeaway from each chapter. It summarizes the message in a short sentence or two to make it easy for you to memorize and think about throughout the day. I also include a Scripture to help you remember God's amazing healing power and promises from the Bible.

You'll notice some of the activities in this book ask you to draw or illustrate an idea. I'm not asking you to become a famous artist—although some of you might discover some hidden talent—but I want you to be able to express yourself to get to the heart of what you see inside of yourself. There are other times I ask you to write about what you feel. There's no right or wrong answer—or picture. Be open and honest with yourself and with God, and you will find what you are looking for.

Once you know what is available through reading *Healing the Soul of a Woman*, reading God's Word, and completing the questions and activities in this book, I pray that you will make a decision to be healed with God's help. The world offers a variety of remedies for the wounds of the soul, and some of them may be helpful, but Jesus offers us complete healing. He is the healer of our souls. The psalmist David said God had restored his soul. When something is restored, it is made like new once again.

What kind of life did God intend for you as a woman who is created in His image? It certainly is not one of being minimized, devalued, mistreated, abused, used, and battered. He offers us unconditional love, infinite worth and value, wholeness, righteousness, peace, and joy—and that is just the beginning of His blessings for those who will believe and walk with Him through life.

I'm so thankful you have decided to take this journey with me! As you begin the journey of healing for your soul, I ask you to remember that healing takes time. It is also sometimes painful, because we have to let old wounds be opened up in order to release the infection that is festering and poisoning our souls. Women who have need of healing for their soul have only two choices. The first is to continue limping along in life, just trying to get through each day. The second is to say, "I've had enough misery, unhappiness, pretense, guilt and shame, and I'm ready to do whatever it takes to be made whole!" I hope you are ready to be healed and whole.

The History of Women

Before you begin, read chapter 1 in *Healing the Soul of a Woman*.

In Touch with Yourself

Jot down some thoughts on what you'd like to learn as you read *Healing the Soul of a Woman* and complete this study guide.

_____

_____

_____

_____

Read the opening quote by Golda Meir. Think about the tiny sparks of possibilities available to you through your dreams, talents, experiences, accomplishments, and the areas of life you are passionate about.

Draw a picture of a fire with flames, and write your tiny sparks on the flames. Write a prayer, asking God to help your sparks grow into flames.

_____

_____

_____

_____

Because of a long history of being devalued and dishonored, many women today, even in places where a lot of progress has been made, still don't see their true worth and value. They doubt their abilities and in many instances won't even try to do great things with their lives simply because of wrong mindsets that are ingrained in them. "I'm just a woman" is a statement that reveals this attitude and is destructive to the soul.

Have you ever felt like you're not enough as a woman? Explain.

_____

_____

_____

What statistics listed in the "Satanic Attacks on Women" section surprise you? Why?

_____

_____

_____

What messages did you receive about being female when you were a child? How did they shape you?

_____

_____

_____

What messages have you heard about being a woman in your adult years? How have they shaped you?

_____

_____

_____

Remember, God knows you are a woman. What has God asked you to do that may not seem conventional in your eyes for a woman?

_____

_____

_____

Evaluate your attitude toward men. Write your general thoughts below.

_____

_____

_____

Evaluate your attitude toward women. Write your general thoughts below.

_____

_____

_____

   Part of the restoration that God offers us is to have a healthy attitude, one that knows when to take a stand against things that are wrong and when to give in and do what someone else is asking us to do. I am so grateful to God that I no longer have to feel like I am fighting the world trying to get what is rightfully mine, and I am thrilled to have this opportunity to teach you that you don't have to do that, either. God wants to fight your battles, and believe me when I say that when God fights on your side, you always win!

Explore God's Word

Read the creation account in Genesis 1–3. Write down your thoughts about what happened.

_____

_____

_____

_____

How does knowing God had a plan for redemption comfort you? (See John 1:4; 3:16.)

_____

_____

_____

_____

Now read Philippians 2:5 regarding our attitude. How can your attitude be like Christ's when it comes to dealing with others?

_____

_____

_____

_____

Healing in Action

What will you do differently this week to have a healthy attitude?

_____

_____

_____

Keep track of your progress by making notes below.

_____

_____

_____

_____

Living the Best Life Available

Before you begin, read chapter 2 in *Healing the Soul of a Woman*.

In Touch with Yourself

How has your attitude become more healthy since working through chapter 1? What other changes would you like to see in your attitude?

_____

_____

_____

_____

Allow your mind to wander and describe what you think "the good life" means. Don't hold back; dream and don't worry about being unrealistic.

_____

_____

_____

_____

If your list is filled with things, remind yourself that there is nothing wrong with having things, but it's important not to confuse *things* with *life*. God offers us true life through Jesus Christ. Now describe true life in Jesus and the difference it has made in your life (or that you would like it to make in your life).

_____

_____

_____

God offers us true life through Jesus Christ—a real life, the best life that anyone can possibly live. He offers us a life of being made right with God, and one of peace and joy (Romans 14:17). Jesus said that He came so that we might have life and that more abundantly (John 10:10).

The best kind of life is only found in God because He is life, and the life that we call ours is a gift from Him. He is the giver of life!

Rate your desire to have an upgrade in your life on a scale from 1 to 10 (with 10 be the most). Why did you choose this rating?

1 2 3 4 5 6 7 8 9 10

_____

_____

_____

_____

How will you invest in achieving the new upgrade? What will you do?

_____

_____

_____

_____

Explore God's Word

Read Ephesians 2:10 from several translations of the Bible. Rewrite the Scripture in your own words below.

_____

_____

_____

_____

Read John 14:6 from several translations. What do you think it means when Jesus says He is the way?

_____

_____

_____

_____

_____

Christianity is not merely belonging to a church and trying to be a good person, but about Jesus and what He has done for us. He offers us Himself as the sacrifice and payment for our sins and guilt, and when we receive Him, He actually comes by His Spirit to live, dwell, and make His home in us. Once you are born again (repent of sin and receive Jesus as Savior), you no longer need to be led by rules and regulations, expecting to get some reward from God if you keep them all, but you can be led and prompted by the Holy Spirit, who will guide you into the full plan of God for your life. It truly is a whole new way of living.

What revelations have you had regarding the "new" way of living during your time as a Christian? How have you upgraded by following the new ways? Which ones still seem hard?

_____

_____

_____

_____

_____

Like learning computer programs, learning the new way can be challenging. It may be tempting to revert to old ways, but if we persist in the new way, it will lead us to greater fruitfulness and ease. Throughout this book I will share many of the new ways that God is offering you, and I sincerely pray that you take advantage of each one of them.

Read Proverbs 4:20–22 NLT and fill in the blanks. Then write in your own words what you think it means.

My _____, pay attention to what I _____.
Listen _____ to my _____. Don't lose
_____ of them. Let them _____ deep into your
_____, for they bring _____ to those who find
them, and _____ to their whole body.

_____

_____

_____

Has God's Word ever literally felt like medicine to your soul? If so, explain.

_____

_____

_____

What areas do you think you need healing in?

_____

_____

_____

What Scriptures can you find that speak to your needs?

_____

_____

_____

Draw an image to symbolize how God's Word is medicine to your soul.
Look at the image often and remember to take your medicine.

The goal of every hurting person is to be healed, and a variety of paths
can be taken. It is very important that you choose a path that is based on
God's Word and His promises; otherwise, you could end up becoming more

and more frustrated as you put time, effort, and perhaps a lot of money into something that never produces any good results. I know people who paid hundreds of thousands of dollars for treatment programs that promised healing and deliverance, and yet they never got any better until they let Jesus into their life and began depending on Him and following His ways.

The important thing is that you make a decision to get the help you need if you are living with wounds and bruises in your soul from past or current situations that need to be healed. An amazing life is waiting for you, one of peace and joy, filled with hope and enthusiasm. It is a life you don't want to miss!

Healing in Action

What are your plans to take steps toward the healing you need?

_____

_____

_____

_____

God Wants the Wounded

Before you begin, read chapter 3 in *Healing the Soul of a Woman.*

In Touch with Yourself

How have you followed through with your plans to begin the healing process?

_____

_____

_____

_____

Read the opening quote by Brennan Manning. What do you think it means? Do you think your wounds resemble anything Jesus went through while He was on earth? Explain.

_____

_____

_____

_____

Take some time to honestly evaluate how much you want to be healed and what you are doing to seek healing. Journal your thoughts.

_____

_____

_____

_____

How open are you to share what you've been through and what you are currently struggling with?

_____

_____

_____

_____

God deliberately chooses those who have been wounded to work in His Kingdom army. He works through their wounds and weaknesses, and people see His power. When people in the world think they are strong and have all the qualifications they need, but they are not leaning and relying on God, He often has to pass them over and instead choose someone who is less qualified from a worldly perspective, but is entirely dependent upon Him in all areas of their life. As you put your trust in God, the day may come when even the people who hurt you will witness the mighty things that God has done in your life and through you as His instrument.

What do you think the statement "Being experienced is a benefit, but getting the experience is painful" means?

_____

_____

_____

_____

Instead of thinking about how much you have gone through in life that has been painful, why not think about all the experience that you now have and all the opportunities that are before you as God's daughter? Remember, with God there are no rejects. That's why Jesus said:

> He who believes in Him [who clings to, trusts in, relies on Him] is not judged [he who trusts in Him never comes up for judgment; for him there is no rejection, no condemnation—he incurs no damnation] . . . (John 3:18).

Explore God's Word

Read Hebrews 5:8–9 from several translations and then write it in your own words.

_____

_____

_____

_____

These two Scripture verses speak volumes to me, not only about Jesus but also about my own life. Jesus needed experience in order to be our High Priest so He could truly say that He understands our pain. My experience with Jesus' healing power qualified me to boldly tell others that Jesus would heal their wounded souls just as He had mine.

Jesus suffered. He gained experience. And it equipped Him for what His Father wanted Him to do. Paul wrote that we have a High Priest who is able "to understand and sympathize and have a shared feeling with our weaknesses," because He has gone through the things we go through now (Hebrews 4:15). I am amazed each time I read and contemplate these Scriptures, and they give me hope that what I have been through will be used to help other people.

Think about what it means to offer your experience to God for His use. Write a prayer, asking God to use you. Be open to hearing what God has to say.

_____

_____

_____

What does it mean that God takes the broken pieces of our lives and makes beautiful things?

_____

_____

_____

Either draw a picture or find a picture that illustrates this concept. Keep it in a place you will see often.

Elisabeth Elliot said, "Of one thing I am sure, God's story never ends with ashes."

That statement touches me deeply and gives me hope. We may begin with ashes, but when we give them to Jesus, He makes something beautiful. Don't let your pain be wasted by being bitter and resentful throughout life because you feel that you have been unjustly treated. Instead, make your experiences a valuable tool for helping others.

Read Isaiah 41:15–17 out loud several times. What do these verses reveal about how God wants to use you as His instrument?

_____

_____

_____

_____

Do you believe there is nothing that has hurt you that God can't heal or restore in your life? Why or why not?

_____

_____

_____

_____

Use the lines below to thank God that *there is nothing you cannot recover from, and nothing that God cannot heal.*

_____

_____

_____

_____

How does it feel to know that you have been sealed by the Holy Spirit, kept safe by God?

_____

_____

_____

You are set apart (sanctified) for God's use, and that includes any and everything that you have gone through that was painful or damaging. I urge you to release all of your past pain and wounds to the Holy Spirit and ask Him to begin His restoration project in your life. Don't waste your pain—let God work it out for your good.

Healing in Action

What ways do you envision God using your pain to help others?

_____

_____

_____

What is one way you can let God use your pain for your good or to help others this week?

_____

_____

_____

CHAPTER 4

What Is a Healthy Soul

Before you begin, read chapter 4 in *Healing the Soul of a Woman*.

In Touch with Yourself

Did you share your testimony with anyone this week? If so, share what happened and how the person responded.

_____

_____

_____

_____

Read the opening Scripture, Psalm 62:1. Do you think your soul finds rest in God? Explain why or why not.

_____

_____

_____

_____

How does focusing on the fact that your salvation comes from God help you find rest?

_____

_____

_____

_____

Imagine that you are able to look into your soul as you look into a mirror. Describe what you see.

_____

_____

_____

_____

Now describe what you'd like your soul to look like.

_____

_____

_____

_____

Jesus is the Prince of Peace, so since He is living in the woman of God, she does indeed have peace at her disposal, yet she may still worry, be anxious, and display emotions that are erratic. To be erratic is to be unstable, unpredictable, inconsistent, changeable, or fitful. Once she decides she no longer wants to live and behave that way, being manipulated by her circumstances, she will begin the process of retraining the emotional part of her soul to come under the guidance of the Holy Spirit that is within her. She will need to rely on God to give her the strength to obey Him, and if she has been fiercely independent, this may take some time and could include several failed attempts at remaining peaceful in the storms of life before she begins to see changes.

What Scriptures and truths can you use to remind yourself that the Holy Spirit lives in you, and He can give you the ability to obey God and remain in His rest?

_____

_____

_____

_____

In order not to become discouraged, it is important to remember that God has promised that He will complete the good work He has begun in us

(Philippians 1:6). Our part is to keep pressing toward the goal and to never give up. Eventually, little by little, our soul will find its rest in God.

Do you agree that you cannot control all of the circumstances in life or the people in your life, but you can control your response to what takes place around you? Explain how this is possible, based on the teaching in chapter 4.

_____

_____

_____

Give yourself a "rest test." Next to each emotion, estimate how much time you allow your mind and soul to be in the conditions described below (use 0 to 100 percent).

Worried or fearful _____

Guilty or ashamed _____

Angry or resentful _____

Anxious about anything _____

Frustrated _____

Wishing your circumstances were different _____

Stressed _____

Nothing is impossible with God, and you can have a supernatural rest that only He can give.

Explore God's Word

Read Matthew 11:28–29 in several translations of the Bible.

Write down the words that stand out to you.

_____

_____

_____

What does Jesus' invitation "Come to Me" say to you? Do you believe it is a personal invitation? Explain.

_____

_____

_____

_____

What does Jesus promise to the heavy-laden and overburdened?

_____

_____

_____

_____

Do you think it is possible for Jesus to deliver what He promises in these verses? Explain.

_____

_____

_____

_____

_____

What does it mean to take Jesus' yoke upon you and learn from Him? How can you do this?

_____

_____

_____

_____

_____

How does Jesus describe Himself in verse 29?

_____

_____

_____

_____

What does Jesus promise you will find in Him?

_____

_____

_____

_____

_____

Reread these verses in The Message paraphrase of the Bible.

Draw or find a picture of what you think the "unforced rhythms of grace" look like.

Healing in Action

Believing (trusting God) is the only doorway into the rest of God. The more we trust God, the easier life becomes because we find that what we commit to Him, He does take care of. He may not do it in our timing or the way we would have, but He does and always will take care of us because He loves us unconditionally.

Make a decision right now to believe God more than you believe how you feel, what you want, or what you think. His promises are greater and more worthy of our trust than anything else. All else is shifting sand, but His Word is lasting and endures forever.

How much do you think you trust God? Rate yourself on a scale from 1 to 10, with 10 being the greatest amount of trust.

1 2 3 4 5 6 7 8 9 10

Now look back over your life and ask yourself how many times God has failed you. Are there examples you can share?

_____

_____

_____

_____

How many times has God taken care of you? Share some examples.

_____

_____

_____

_____

Based on your experiences, write the reasons you should trust God completely, all the time.

_____

_____

_____

_____

When you are tempted to handle things your way or to follow your emotions rather than trust God, reread your reasons for trusting God.

CHAPTER 5

Help Me! I Don't Understand Myself

Before you begin, read chapter 5 in *Healing the Soul of a Woman*.

In Touch with Yourself

Have you taken your reasons to trust God to heart this week? What were the results? Would you give yourself a better rating now?

_____

_____

_____

_____

Read the opening quote by Thales. What do you think about it?

_____

_____

_____

_____

Have you ever done things and wondered why you did them? Explain.

_____

_____

_____

_____

Do you say things you wish you hadn't or think things you wish you wouldn't? Explain.

_____

_____

_____

_____

Do you believe there is a reason for your behavior, thoughts, or words? Explain.

_____

_____

_____

_____

Learning to understand the root of our behaviors is vital to changing them. Studying God's Word helps us gain insight. It may reveal to us that we have a root of fear in our lives that is affecting our actions and reactions.

Take some time today to reflect on your behaviors, words, and thoughts, especially the ones you do not like, and pray about them. Ask God to reveal the root of what's really going on. (If you find this extremely hard to do, you may consider talking to a trusted friend or even a trained professional to help uncover some of the reasons.)

Write down some of the things you need to pray about and ask God to help you.

_____

_____

_____

I recommend that when you have a bad or unusual reaction to a person or situation, instead of rushing past it, take time to ponder it and ask God to help you understand why you behaved as you did. Doing this has greatly helped me to get to the root of problems in my life.

Do you believe the statement "You cannot do anything about something if you are blind to it"? Explain.

_____

_____

_____

Explore God's Word

Read Psalm 119:105. Share how God's Word can be a light to your path.

_____

_____

_____

_____

_____

Read Psalm 119:124–125. Why do you think the psalmist wants discernment?

_____

_____

_____

_____

Have you asked God for discernment? Why or why not? Consider praying for discernment now and write your prayer below.

_____

_____

_____

_____

If we don't face truth, we will not be free from the things that steal our peace and joy. Discernment requires that we slow down and think more deeply in order to get to the root of our behaviors. Finding out why we do what we do is very valuable. Sometimes it takes a crisis to wake us up and help us see in ourselves what others see.

Read Psalm 139 from several versions of the Bible. Then write what stands out to you.

_____

_____

_____

_____

Healing in Action

Have you read books or articles about your personality type? If so, describe what you've learned about yourself. If not, consider taking a personality test or reading a book to help you find out which type you are.

_____

_____

_____

_____

What are some ways you can find out more about your personality? What will you commit to do this week?

_____

_____

_____

_____

What do you know about your personality already (likes and dislikes, your temperament and the way you express yourself)?

_____

_____

_____

_____

What do you consider as strengths of your personality or temperament?

_____

_____

_____

_____

What do you consider to be weaknesses of your personality or temperament?

_____

_____

_____

_____

Learn all you can about yourself and it will help you become your true self. I think we all have a pretend self, one that we project to the world, but God wants us to be our true self, the person He created us to be.

You don't have to wait for a crisis in your life to begin your journey of healing and wholeness. The sooner you begin, the happier you will be.

You Are God's Beloved

Before you begin, read chapter 6 in *Healing the Soul of a Woman*.

In Touch with Yourself

Have you discovered more about your personality type? If so, what have you learned about your strengths and weaknesses?

_____

_____

_____

_____

Read the opening Scripture from 1 John 3:2 out loud. Then write down what this verse says to you.

_____

_____

_____

_____

Describe what unconditional love looks like to you. You may even draw any pictures that come to mind.

_____

_____

_____

_____

_____

_____

_____

_____

Have you experienced the unconditional love of God? Explain.

_____

_____

_____

What does it mean to be the beloved of God? It is a term of affection and endearment, and it means to long for, to respect and hold in affectionate regard. As I pondered the word *beloved*, I sensed that it means to be loved, or the thought of being loved at every moment in time. Just think about it: You are being loved right now and at every moment. There never has been and never will be a moment in time when you are not being perfectly loved.

I suggest you stop reading, close your eyes, and let your soul get quiet. Now say out loud, "I am God's beloved." Say it a few times and let it impact your soul. I believe this exercise could be very impactful, especially if you have never really believed that you are loved or have felt loved.

Explore God's Word

Read the following Scriptures that use the terms *loved* or *beloved*. Write down what these verses mean to you.

Matthew 3:17

_____

_____

_____

_____

1 John 4:10–11

_____

_____

_____

_____

1 John 4:18

_____

_____

_____

_____

Don't be discouraged if it takes a while for you to fully grasp the thought of being loved unconditionally by God. Our experience has taught us that love seems to ebb and flow based on the moods of people and whether or not we are giving them what they want from us. We quickly fall into a pattern of trying to earn love by making people happy and fearing that love may be lost if we don't please them. People love us imperfectly, but God's love is perfect because He is perfect. He is love, and therefore, it is impossible for Him to ever do anything less than love us unconditionally.

Write a letter to God in response to His unconditional love for you.

_____

_____

_____

Healing in Action

If you have any doubts about God's love, share them with Him. You may want to jot down your thoughts below.

_____

_____

_____

Read aloud Ephesians 3:17–19. Use these verses as your prayer to ask God to reveal His amazing love to you.

Be intentional about noticing how God loves you this week. Write down any experiences that reveal His love for you. (Feel free to use more paper when needed.)

_____

_____

_____

We miss out on so much in our relationship with God because we try to "get" what He wants us to have instead of simply receiving it by faith. To *get* means you obtain something by struggle and effort. We cannot "get" God to love us because He already does, and He always will. He declares that He loves you with an everlasting love (Jeremiah 31:3). That is a love that cannot come to an end. So please believe in and receive God's love. And on those days when you make huge mistakes or have big problems and Satan, the enemy of your soul, tries to separate you from God's love, open up your Bible and read these verses (and write them here in your own words).
Romans 8:35

_____

_____

_____

Romans 8:38–39

_____

_____

_____

Hurting People Hurt People

Before you begin, read chapter 7 in *Healing the Soul of a Woman*.

In Touch with Yourself

Where have you seen God's love in action this week?

_____

_____

_____

_____

_____

Read the opening Scripture from Romans 12:19. You may want to read it from several different versions. Now write what this verse means to you.

_____

_____

_____

_____

_____

How does it make you feel to know that vengeance is God's and not yours?

_____

_____

_____

_____

_____

Do you think it is difficult to forgive people who have hurt you? Why or why not?

_____

_____

_____

_____

_____

Describe a time you have forgiven a person. How did you do it? How do you feel now that you have forgiven that person?

_____

_____

_____

_____

_____

Is there someone you have not forgiven yet? If so, why?

_____

_____

_____

_____

_____

Do you believe that hurting people hurt other people? Explain why or why not.

_____

_____

_____

_____

_____

On your journey of healing, possibly the most difficult thing that God will ask you to do is forgive the people who hurt you. It certainly was very challenging for me. One of the things that helped me a lot was when God showed me that hurting people hurt other people. We normally only think of how much we are hurting and then proceed to be angry with the people who have hurt us, but most of the time they are hurting, too.

Someone or something has hurt them, and they are acting out of their own pain, often not even realizing their actions are hurting others.

Do you believe that forgiving those who have hurt you is one of the most powerful things you can do? Explain.

_____

_____

_____

I believe that for many women, hanging on to anger and refusing to forgive those who have hurt them stands in the way of their healing. We cannot go forward if we are bitterly hanging on to the past.

Explore God's Word

Read the parable of the unmerciful servant in Matthew 18:21–35. Write down anything that stands out to you in this story.

_____

_____

_____

Now think of someone you are having a tough time forgiving and rewrite the parable using your relationship with God as the first scenario of a debt forgiven, and the situation with that person as the second scenario of a debt that needs to be forgiven.

_____

_____

_____

_____

_____

_____

Draw a picture showing the cycle of forgiveness God wants us to use, according to the parable.

What Scriptures from today's chapter stand out to you?

_____

_____

_____

_____

Which ones can help you with forgiveness?

_____

_____

_____

_____

It is very important for anyone reading this book who is in need of healing for a wounded soul to take this command from God seriously. Don't decide to rush past this chapter because you have already decided that you just can't forgive the people who hurt you because it is too hard. Forgiving our enemies is nonnegotiable for anyone who wants to enjoy the promise of God for restoration. It is something God teaches us to do, and it is something that Jesus modeled in His own life. Jesus prayed, while suffering on the cross, that His crucifiers would be forgiven. He knew that they were hurting Him out of their own hurt and confusion.

Healing in Action

Reread the words of Nelson Mandela in this chapter. What do you think he meant when he said he wanted to be free, so he forgave those who had wronged him?

_____

_____

_____

_____

How can his words help you forgive others?

_____

_____

_____

_____

Perhaps it is time for you to get to the root cause of some of the problems that you deal with, rather than merely continuing to treat symptoms that never completely go away. Getting to the root of our problems is what the healing of the soul is all about. We open ourselves up to God and let Him into all the areas of our lives, and we trust Him to guide us through the process of restoration and wholeness. When things are brought out into the light, they lose their power over us. The Bible says that when anything is exposed and reproved by the light, it is made visible and clear (Ephesians 5:13).

Making the decision to forgive your enemies is the first step, and when you do that you can begin to deal with the anger you have from the unjust things that have happened to you. We can let go of bitterness and anger and replace them with trust in God and hope for the future.

How can you go a step further and bless those who have hurt you?

_____

_____

_____

_____

Commit to praying for those who have hurt you today. Then commit to doing at least one thing to bless them. Write down your plans and then journal about how it affected you after you blessed that person or people.

_____

_____

_____

_____

Remember

When we obey God, He always brings a reward.

But love your enemies, do good to them, and lend to them without expecting to get anything back. Then your reward will be great, and you will be children of the Most High, because he is kind to the ungrateful and wicked (Luke 6:35 NIV).

Not Guilty and Unashamed

Before you begin, read chapter 8 in *Healing the Soul of a Woman*.

In Touch with Yourself

What did you do to bless someone who has hurt you in the past? What happened? How did it impact your life?

_____

_____

_____

_____

Read the opening verse from Isaiah 54:4 out loud. Write down five words that first come to mind when you hear this verse.

_____

_____

_____

_____

Do you have feelings of guilt and shame? If so, write about them. Why do you feel this way?

_____

_____

_____

_____

Think about this statement: *People don't abuse you, misuse you, or even mistreat you because there is something wrong with you; they do it because there is something wrong with them.* Do you believe this is true? Explain.

_____

_____

_____

_____

If you are loaded down with guilt and shame, it is time for you to take a stand and draw a line in the sand, so to speak, and refuse to continue the way you have been living. If there are things in the past that you are sorry for, repent and receive forgiveness from God and get on with your life. If you have been abused in any way, forgive those who hurt you and get on with your life. But don't continue merely feeling guilty and ashamed. It is time for a new beginning. Your past does not have any power over your present moment unless you allow it to.

Write a letter to yourself, releasing you from any guilt and shame in your soul. You may even consider writing what you think God would say to you—He is your loving Father.

_____

_____

_____

_____

There are only two ways that guilt can settle in your soul and torment you. The first is if you have done something wrong and never asked for forgiveness, and the second is if you have asked for but not received the mercy and forgiveness that God offers us. When sin is forgiven, it is removed as far as east is from west (Psalm 103:12) and there is nothing left to feel guilty about; therefore, any feelings of guilt should be resisted. The feeling may be real, but it is based on a lie, not a reality. When God forgives us, He remembers our sin no more (Isaiah 43:25), and surely, if He can forget our wrongdoing, we can, too. The Bible is very clear that Jesus took our transgressions and guilt upon Himself, and since He took them, we don't have them any longer.

Explore God's Word

Meditate on Psalm 103:12. How far is the east from the west? Draw a picture illustrating how far God has removed our transgressions from us.

Read Isaiah 53:5 from several versions of the Bible. Write what Christ's sacrifice means for us, according to this verse.

_____

_____

_____

_____

Read 2 Corinthians 5:21. What does it say about what happened to you when you accepted Christ as your Savior?

_____

_____

_____

_____

Write a prayer of thanks for what God has done for you through Jesus Christ.

_____

_____

_____

_____

The mere fact that you know a Scripture about right standing with God or have heard someone teach on righteousness with God does not mean that it has become a reality in your life. I often tell people that we really don't fully know or have revelation of any of God's truths until we can see that they are working in our lives. When you truly believe that you have been made right with God through faith in Christ, you will stop feeling guilty, condemned, and ashamed.

If you still suffer a lot with feelings of guilt and shame, you still need more revelation about who you are in Christ. No matter how long it takes, please don't get discouraged and give up. Giving up is exactly what Satan wants you to do, but God wants you to keep pressing into His truth. Continue studying about your right standing with God and confess it often, and the day will come when the reality of it will make its way from your head to your heart. Once it is firmly established in you, then when the devil comes against you, he will never defeat you.

Healing in Action

Now that you have released guilt and shame and read about how God views you, write an affirmation you can repeat often to remind yourself of who you are in Christ.

_____

_____

_____

_____

Declare the truth about who you are in Christ often.

After over forty years of studying and teaching God's Word, I still confess each day that I am the righteousness of God in Christ. Doing so reminds me of who I am in Jesus, and confessing His Word defends and protects me from the lies of Satan.

Even if you are not where you want to be in your walk with God, you don't have to feel guilty and ashamed. You can rejoice that you have made some progress. Jesus, who began a good work in you, will complete it. He will continue developing and perfecting His work in us right up to the time of Christ's return (Philippians 1:6). When the devil attacks you with guilt and shame you can say, "I may not be where I need to be, but thank God I am not where I used to be. God is working in me right now, and each day I am making more progress!"

Write your testimony—a short description of what God has done for you or how far God has brought you on this journey. Review and update it often to help you focus on the progress you're making, rather than how far you have to go.

_____

_____

_____

_____

Remember

Keep reminding yourself that the devil is a liar and replace his lies with God's Word.

Let the redeemed of the LORD tell their story (Psalm 107:2 NIV).

Finding Your True Self

Before you begin, read chapter 9 in *Healing the Soul of a Woman*.

In Touch with Yourself

How has the chapter helped you to declare who you are in Christ this last week?

_____

_____

_____

_____

Read the opening Scripture from 2 Corinthians 5:17. What does it mean to be a new creation? What specific ways have you been made new?

_____

_____

_____

_____

Take an honest inventory of yourself. Do you know who you are? If so, write a short description. If not, explore ways you can learn who you truly are, according to what God says about you.

_____

_____

_____

_____

Chameleons are lizards that have an ability to change colors in order to blend into their surroundings. They do this to protect themselves from predators, and although we cannot change colors, we do sometimes develop false identities, hoping to protect ourselves from rejection or disapproval.

Have you ever behaved like a chameleon—changing your "colors" to blend into your surroundings? Describe how.

_____

_____

_____

_____

_____

Now ask yourself why you felt the need to change.

_____

_____

_____

_____

_____

Was it worth it? Explain why or why not.

_____

_____

_____

_____

_____

When we receive Jesus as our Savior, according to Scripture, we are born again, or born anew. It is a point in our lives where we are invited to let go of anything old and fully become the amazing person that God originally intended us to be before our experience with the world and sin wounded us. Our sins are forgiven, and we have an opportunity to receive God's unconditional love and mercy. We are made new, and life is filled with possibility. I like to say that we become new spiritual clay, and by allowing the Holy

Spirit to mold us, rather than letting the world do it, we can become our true selves.

How has the Holy Spirit changed your life, or molded you, thus far? Draw an illustration that represents the way you've changed.

Explore God's Word

Think about the statement "God will never help you to be someone else." What does that mean for you? How does it impact your understanding of His love for you?

_____

_____

_____

_____

_____

_____

God has gifted you to be able to do something special, but it may not be what other people are doing. Take some time and search your heart to discover what you love, and then find the courage in Christ to do it. Even if what you desire to do is something that has never been done before, remember that there is always someone who is the first at everything.

Fill in the blank for each Scripture, then write what it means to you as you step out in faith and find the courage to do what your heart loves.

For God has not given us a _____ of _____ and
_____, but of _____, _____, and
_____. (2 Timothy 1:7 NLT)

_____

_____

_____

I can do _____ things through _____ which
_____ me. (Philippians 4:13 KJV)

_____

_____

_____

If you _____ in me and my _____ remain in
you, _____ whatever you _____, and it will be
done for _____. (John 15:7 NIV)

_____

_____

_____

Have I not commanded you? Be _____ and _____.
Do not be _____; do not be _____, for
the LORD your _____ will be with you wherever you
_____. (Joshua 1:9 NIV)

_____

_____

_____

Choose at least one of these Scriptures (or another one) to memorize and repeat daily.

Answer the following questions:

Have you found your sweet spot in life? If so, what is it?

_____

_____

_____

Are you comfortable being you? Why or why not?

_____

_____

_____

How much do you compare yourself with others and perhaps try to become someone you are not? Explain.

_____

_____

_____

Asking these questions may be the beginning of finding your true self and becoming the you that God created you to be!

Celebrate the woman God has created you to be, and be you!

Healing in Action

Reread the words of Henri Nouwen: "Over the years, I have come to realize that the greatest trap in our life is not success, popularity, or power, but self-rejection. Self-rejection is the greatest enemy of the spiritual life because it contradicts the sacred voice that calls us the Beloved."

Do you agree or disagree with these statements? Explain.

_____

_____

_____

_____

How is rejecting ourselves contradictory to the sacred voice of God, the One who calls us beloved?

_____

_____

_____

_____

_____

Meditate on the fact that God calls you beloved. Write down five words to describe what it means to you to be God's beloved.

_____

_____

_____

_____

_____

Our true self is one who is the beloved of God. Every other identity is a false one. If we know we are God's beloved, it gives us confidence to step into our true destiny, whatever that may be. It may be to sew and grow a garden, or it may be to travel the world preaching the Gospel. But whatever our true destiny is, it isn't nearly as important as us being comfortable with what it is. In order to find healing for our souls, it is important to allow the Word of God to define us rather than allowing the world to define us. When our time in this world comes to an end, the only opinion that will matter is God's, so don't waste your life being overly concerned about what other people think of you.

Using Scripture, write declarations that will remind you that you are God's beloved. Repeat them daily and ask God to give you revelation of what these truths mean for you.

_____

_____

_____

_____

Remember

You are a new creature in Christ, and you are His beloved—unique, treasured, valued and desired by God Himself.

But you are a chosen people, a royal priesthood, a holy nation, God's special possession, that you may declare the praises of him who called you out of darkness into his wonderful light (1 Peter 2:9 NIV).

No Parking at Any Time

Before you begin, read chapter 10 of *Healing the Soul of a Woman*.

In Touch with Yourself

Are you learning to refuse and overcome self-rejection more? Write about any changes you have experienced.

_____

_____

_____

_____

Read the opening Scripture. Why do you think God told Moses to command the people to go forward?

_____

_____

_____

_____

What does moving forward look like in your life?

_____

_____

_____

_____

You are probably reading this book because something or someone has wounded you in the past, and I want to encourage you not to park your life, dreams, and goals at the place of your pain and just give up on life. Keep going forward. God created us to be people who are always moving forward. Being successful in anything isn't a one-time achievement, but rather a continual state of being.

Where have you parked your life (either now or in the past)?

_____

_____

_____

_____

_____

How can you begin, or continue, to put one foot in front of the other so you can move forward in life?

_____

_____

_____

_____

What historical person have you learned about who kept going despite overwhelming odds and setbacks? How can that person's story inspire you to keep going?

_____

_____

_____

_____

_____

History is full of people who overcame the overwhelming odds and setbacks life threw their way. Helen Keller lost her sight and hearing, but she accomplished great things in spite of her disabilities. Franklin Roosevelt's paralysis could have defeated him, but he pressed on and served in the nation's highest office as president. History is filled with stories of ordinary people who accomplished extraordinary things because they didn't park their life at the point of their pain.

Explore God's Word

Use a Bible app or concordance to look up some of the tragedies that the apostle Paul went through. Write down what happened to him, how he responded, and what you can learn from the way Paul handled the situation.

_____

_____

_____

_____

Read God's promise to Abram in Genesis 12.

Now read about Abram's father, Terah, in Genesis 11:27–35.

Do you think Terah achieved all he could, or did he park his life? What do you think may have happened if he had kept going?

_____

_____

_____

_____

Do you ever feel like you have not completed something that God has called you to do? Explain.

_____

_____

_____

_____

How can the stories of Terah and Abram inspire you to keep moving forward?

_____

_____

_____

_____

Perhaps you are facing a time of testing in your life right now and the temptation to quit and give up is strong. Know this: You have what it takes to go through it and experience victory because God is on your side.

We often try to leap over our problems or find a way to go around them so we don't have to deal with them, but that never produces good results in our life. We might avoid dealing with them for a long time, but they will remain in our way until we find the courage to go through them. If we hope to see the end fulfillment of our dreams, we need to go all the way through the things that are blocking our path. We cannot go part of the way and then park when life is difficult.

This week, read the story of Ruth (found in the book of Ruth). Spend time focusing on how Ruth refused to park when life got tough. How did she move forward? How can you move forward?

_____

_____

_____

_____

Healing in Action

Make a determined decision to remove the parking signs in your life. You can even replace them with "no parking" signs so you'll be mindful to keep moving forward.

Create a sign on a separate sheet of paper to remind yourself to move forward a little more each day. Post it in a place you will see it often.

New beginnings and fresh starts are never in short supply with God. You may feel forgotten and worn out, but God has not forgotten you. New and exciting things are waiting for you—all you need to do to get started in your new life is get up and keep on going. Here is God's promise for you. Hang on to it and don't look back!

> Do not [earnestly] remember the former things; neither consider the things of old. Behold, I am doing a *new* thing! (Isaiah 43:18–19, emphasis mine).

Remember

Make the right decision—the decision to press past your pain and enjoy all that God has planned for you.

"For I know the plans I have for you," declares the Lord, "plans to prosper you and not to harm you, plans to give you hope and a future" (Jeremiah 29:11 NIV).

You Are Not Damaged Goods

Before you begin, read chapter 11 in *Healing the Soul of a Woman*.

In Touch with Yourself

Have you removed any parking signs in your life? How are you moving forward?

_____

_____

_____

Read the opening Scripture, Colossians 2:10. Read it again from several translations, and then write what it means to you.

_____

_____

_____

Do you believe you are complete? Explain why or why not.

_____

_____

_____

Do you believe that God wants you to do meaningful or purpose-filled things? Explain why or why not.

_____

_____

_____

Don't despair: God will meet you where you are and help you get to where you need to be.

Read my testimony at the beginning of this chapter. Have you ever felt like you were damaged goods like I did? If so, explain.

_____

_____

_____

_____

Have you experienced healing in your soul yet? Explain why or why not.

_____

_____

_____

_____

If you haven't received healing, stop right now. Pour your heart out to God and ask Him to help you. Write down your prayer or any thoughts that come to you as you pray.

_____

_____

_____

_____

Do you know of anyone you can pray with or talk to as you go through the healing process? Write their names below and contact them today.

_____

_____

_____

_____

When we put ourselves in God's healing hands, we may begin broken and damaged, but we end up whole and complete, without any evidence we were ever marred. When I talk about the way I used to be, I feel like I am talking about someone I once knew who is now only a vague memory.

If we realize that we are made complete in Christ, we never have to believe we are damaged and have to settle for second best in life. To be complete in Christ means that whatever we might be lacking, He makes up for it. His strength shows itself in our weakness (2 Corinthians 12:9); our sin is swallowed up by His mercy and forgiveness. Our past disappears in the light of the new life He offers us.

Explore God's Word

Read the biblical account of Daniel's friends Shadrach, Meshach, and Abednego (Daniel 3).

Write a brief description of their story in Daniel 3.

_____

_____

_____

_____

Now reread Daniel 3:27. How does this verse describe the outcome of their deliverance?

_____

_____

_____

_____

You can come out of the fiery furnace of life, and there will be no evidence you were ever in it. Not even the smell of the life you once lived will cling to you. You are not damaged goods, and I urge you not to think that you are. Don't plan for a second-rate life, but instead plan on an amazing life in which you do amazing things.

Read what happened to Saul's grandson Mephibosheth in 2 Samuel 4:4. Describe his situation below.

_____

_____

_____

Now read what David did for him (2 Samuel 9). How does this compare to what God wants to do for you and your wounded soul?

_____

_____

_____

_____

Have you been living an inferior life because you have a poor self-image? Explain.

_____

_____

_____

_____

Do you feel worthless, damaged, or as if it is too late for you? Explain.

_____

_____

_____

_____

From that day forward David provided everything that Mephibosheth and his young son Mica needed, and the Bible says he ate continually at the king's table even though he was lame in both feet (2 Samuel 9:13). I love that part. It helps me realize that even though we are lame (have weaknesses), we can still eat at the table of our King Jesus.

Have you been crawling around under the table, being satisfied with the crumbs that fall on the floor? Have you settled for less than God's best? Imagine how you would feel if you prepared a wonderful meal and called your children to come and eat, and they all got under the table and began to tell you how worthless they were and that they were not qualified to sit at the table. That is how God feels when we refuse to receive His blessings because we believe we are damaged and therefore not worth anything. Jesus paid a high price for our healing and restoration when He died on the cross, so let's start receiving the benefits He purchased for us with His sacrifice.

Healing in Action

Allow yourself to daydream about what it looks like to "eat at the King's table." Write about it or draw a picture.

_____

_____

_____

Embrace the truth that you are not damaged goods. You are God's beloved and can live the life He has created for you!

Remember

You don't have to sacrifice anymore because Jesus has done it for you—now you can sit at the table and eat with the King!

> The thief's purpose is to steal and kill and destroy. My purpose is to give them a rich and satisfying life (John 10:10 NLT).

The Wounds of Sin

Before you begin, read chapter 12 in *Healing the Soul of a Woman.*

In Touch with Yourself

How has this impacted your healing process to realize the truth that you are *not* damaged goods? Explain.

_____

_____

_____

_____

Read the opening Scripture from Psalm 38:5. What do you think the verse means?

_____

_____

_____

_____

Read Julie's story. Do you have any unconfessed sins that have damaged you and your family or others? Explain.

_____

_____

_____

_____

Read my suggestions for dealing with your sin and write down any thoughts you may have about your personal situation.

_____

_____

_____

_____

Talk to God openly about your past. Read the story of David and Bathsheba in 2 Samuel 11, then read his prayer of repentance in Psalm 51.

Don't ever be so afraid of the light that you choose to remain in darkness. Although David had ignored his sin for a long time, it is obvious from his confession that he felt the weight of it. Perhaps he stayed so busy that he did not have to deal with it, or he may have made excuses for it—at least I know that is what I have often done in the past to avoid dealing with my own wrong behavior. Another way we may avoid dealing with our sin is to blame it on someone else. We may have ourselves convinced that if they hadn't done what they did, then we wouldn't have done what we did. Although there may be a grain of truth in that kind of thinking, we will never be free from the burden of sin unless we take responsibility for it and bring it out into the open—first with God and then, if necessary, with people.

Receive the forgiveness you have asked for. Do you really believe God has forgiven you of the sin you have confessed?

_____

_____

_____

_____

Talk openly with the people you have wounded. Who do you need to share your heart with—even if they do not readily accept your apology?

_____

_____

_____

_____

Write a prayer, asking God to bless and help those you have wounded.

_____

_____

_____

Show love to those you have wounded. Read 1 Peter 4:8. What does it mean to you?

_____

_____

_____

When we continue to be kind and loving to those who are hardened against us, it will eventually have a wonderful healing effect on them.

You will need to be patient, because it will probably take time for the people we have hurt to believe we have changed and are truly sorry. We need to remember that just as our wounds have taken time to heal, theirs will, also.

Explore God's Word

Read Romans 8:1 and John 3:17. Why is there no condemnation in Christ?

_____

_____

_____

I believe it was important for me to stop carrying the blame in order for God to work in the situation. If you are carrying blame from something you have done in the past, I urge you to release it and realize that although you cannot go back and undo something you have done that hurt someone else, there is nothing that is impossible for God. He can change the heart of the one you hurt and heal the wounds you both have.

When we have deeply hurt someone, it is very difficult to release the burden of our actions, but it truly is the only thing we can do in order to go on with life.

What other verses from the Bible can remind you to release guilt and shame once you have asked for forgiveness?

_____

_____

_____

Letting go of the past may be hard to do, but it is much better than reliving it every day of your life.

Be careful about thinking and saying that the things God asks you to do are too hard. God gives us His Spirit to do hard and difficult things, to do things that people who live without God in their lives are not able to do. Too frequently, I hear people say, "I know what God wants me to do, but it is just too hard." I also see them continue to live lives that are unhappy and unfulfilling.

Being convinced that doing God's will is too hard often causes people to backslide in their commitment to Christ. At one time they fully intended to obey the Lord, but when He asked them to do something that was difficult, they decided it was just too hard and went back to their old way of living. Many of the disciples who once followed Jesus turned back to their old way of life when He asked them to do things that they perceived as being too hard (see John 6:60–66). God never asks us to do anything unless He enables us to do it. He wants us to believe and take steps of faith, and when we do, we will discover that with God all things are possible!

Healing in Action

Jesus became our substitute—He has suffered and has been punished for our sins. He was wounded for our transgressions. His wounds have healed our wounds, but that only becomes a reality in our life when we believe it and let go of the past.

You can trust God with all the mistakes of your past. He is able to heal and save to the uttermost (Hebrews 7:25). No one is beyond His reach—not you, and not the people you may have hurt.

Journal about (or draw an illustration of) Jesus serving as your substitute. How does that impact the sin in your life? What is the effect in your soul-healing process?

_____

_____

_____

Remember

No one is beyond His reach—not you, and not the people you may have hurt.

Therefore He is able also to save to the uttermost (completely, perfectly, finally, and for all time and eternity) those who come to God through Him, since He is always living to make petition to God *and* intercede with Him *and* intervene for them (Hebrews 7:25 AMPC).

Learning to Live Inside Out

Before you begin, read chapter 13 in *Healing the Soul of a Woman*.

In Touch with Yourself

How has remembering that Jesus serves as your substitute helped you in your journey toward healing? Explain.

_____

_____

_____

Read the opening Scripture from Galatians 2:20. What words stand out to you in the verse? What does it mean to you?

_____

_____

_____

What happens when we accept Christ as our Savior? Explain the amazing work He does in us and how it affects us.

_____

_____

_____

We receive His righteousness, His peace, His joy, and the fruit of His Spirit. We are justified in Him, redeemed in Him, and sanctified in Him. We have the mind of Christ, we are forgiven, we are dead to sin—and this is only the beginning of what God's Word says that we are and have in Christ.

Have you learned, like Paul did, to put your trust in Jesus for everything, rather than putting it in yourself or others? Explain why or why not.

_____

_____

_____

Read the list below of what you get when you receive Jesus. Put a check next to the ones you have believed and experienced and an *x* next to those you have not.

_____ *You are complete in Christ.*

_____ *You are alive with Christ.*

_____ *You are free from the law of sin and death.*

_____ *You are far from oppression, and do not fear, for terror does not come near you.*

_____ *You are born of God, and the evil one does not touch you.*

_____ *You are holy and without blame before the Lord.*

_____ *You have the mind of Christ.*

_____ *You have the peace of God that surpasses your understanding.*

_____ *You have the Greater One living in you, and He is greater than your enemy who is in the world.*

_____ *You have received the gift of righteousness and reign in life with Christ.*

All of the amazing things that become ours in Christ are quite astounding. We begin our walk with God by believing His promises are true, and only then will we begin to experience the reality of them in our daily lives. Most of the time people say, "I'll believe that when I see it," but God's promises must be believed first. Believe in your heart first and see later.

Faith and patience are the keys that unlock the vault to God's promises (Hebrews 6:12).

Explore God's Word

Reread your checklist. Look up the Scriptures found in the book next to the ones you need to receive by faith. Write what those verses say in your own words, what they mean for you.

_____

_____

_____

_____

Use a study Bible and look up the verses referenced next to these verses. What do they say?

_____

_____

_____

_____

Countless Scripture verses speak of us being in Christ. One of them is found in Philippians 3:3, which says that our confidence is to be *in Christ* and not in our own ability to perform. We learn to find our worth and value in Him instead of in our own works or what we can do. Confidence is important, and I dedicate an entire chapter to it later in the book, but let me encourage you to never put your confidence in things that are shaky. Jesus is the Rock that we can depend on, and He is completely dependable.

Rewrite Philippians 3:3 in your own words.

_____

_____

_____

_____

Picture Jesus making a deposit in you. What do you find? Journal about it or draw an illustration.

_____

_____

_____

Reread Psalm 139 and write what stands out to you.

_____

_____

_____

_____

Compare your notes to what you wrote in chapter 5 of this workbook. Do you see any changes? Similarities?

_____

_____

_____

_____

Healing in Action

If we live, dwell, and remain in Him, and let His Word (Jesus) live, dwell, and remain in us, God's Word promises us that we will bear much good fruit (John 15:5). When we become Christians, we don't begin a journey of behavior modification, but one of learning to "do life" with Jesus. To live, dwell, and remain in Him simply means to fellowship with Him, lean on Him, trust in Him, rely on Him, learn His Word, and talk to Him about everything all the time. He is our source of all good things, and that certainly includes good behavior on our part. Learn to live inside out and your behavior will become more and more like Jesus'. Focus more on who you are in Christ, rather than struggling to modify your behavior.

Do you spend more time trying to modify your behavior or focusing on who you are in Christ? Explain

_____

_____

_____

_____

How can you focus more on who you are in Christ? What Scriptures will help you do this each day?

_____

_____

_____

_____

Remember

Trust God's grace to work in you continually, enabling you to be all that He wants you to be.

I can do all things because Christ gives me the strength (Philippians 4:13 NLV).

You've Got What It Takes

Before you begin, read chapter 14 from *Healing the Soul of a Woman*.

In Touch with Yourself

Have you focused more on who you are in Christ? What changes have you noticed?

_____

_____

_____

_____

Read Philippians 4:13 from several versions. Choose a version to memorize and write it below.

_____

_____

_____

_____

Do you believe you can do anything because God lives in you? Explain why or why not.

_____

_____

_____

_____

What challenge or struggle do you need to give to God so you can receive His strength to do what you need to do?

_____

_____

_____

_____

Don't ever forget that what you believe will become your reality. No matter how many wonderful things Jesus has done for us or deposited in us, they won't help us unless we firmly believe they are ours. Let's always remember that the devil is a liar, and if we believe his lies, then we become deceived, just as Eve was in the beginning of time. Learning to believe and trust God's Word more than we believe what we think or feel makes the difference in living victoriously or being defeated.

What should you say to yourself when you feel you cannot do something?

_____

_____

_____

_____

What do you think it means to be more than a conqueror in Christ (Romans 8:37)?

_____

_____

_____

_____

Do you believe you are more than a conqueror? Explain why or why not.

_____

_____

_____

_____

Write a prayer now asking God to increase your faith and help you see yourself as a conqueror.

_____

_____

_____

_____

Explore God's Word

Read Romans 8:28–39. Circle the words that remind you that you can do all things through Christ. Write those words here.

_____

_____

_____

_____

The devil delights in making us think we are weak and incapable, but the truth is that we have all of God's strength available to us. We may be weak in ourselves, but His strength shows itself most effective through our weakness when we lean on and rely on Him.

Read Paul's story in 2 Corinthians 12:1–10. What happened to him?

_____

_____

_____

_____

How did he deal with the thorn in his flesh?

_____

_____

_____

_____

If God simply removed every difficulty from our lives, there would be no need for Him in our daily lives. He leaves a certain amount of weakness in each of us in order to have a place to show Himself strong. He wants to be needed. He wants to be sought after. He wants us to believe that we can do whatever we need to do through Him.

Healing in Action

Do you see yourself as a victim, a survivor, or one who is more than a conqueror in Christ? Explain.

_____

_____

_____

_____

_____

What can you do to see more clearly the truth of who you are in Christ and what He's done in you?

_____

_____

_____

_____

_____

I believe that as long as we see ourselves as victims, we continue to feel victimized and often carry resentment about our past. However, in Christ, our past does not need to determine our future.

Likewise, I believe that if we see ourselves as mere survivors, it still leaves us with thoughts of being someone who has barely come through a tragedy instead of someone who is strong and an overcomer. I never refer to myself as a victim of incest or as a survivor of it. I am a new creature in Christ, and so are you if you believe in Jesus.

How we see ourselves and what we believe are extremely important.

Draw a picture of how you see yourself. Revisit this picture often throughout the course of this study, noticing any differences you have as you continue to grow in Christ.

Remember

You are not weak; you are strong. You are more than a conqueror through Jesus. You are an overcomer!

> No, in all these things we are more than conquerors through him who loved us (Romans 8:37 NIV).

Roadblocks to Healing

Before you begin, read chapter 15 in *Healing the Soul of a Woman*.

In Touch with Yourself

How has envisioning yourself as "more than a conqueror" helped you on the road to healing? Explain.

_____

_____

_____

_____

Now read the opening Scripture from Isaiah 57:14. What obstacles do you think still stand in the way of you living a completely whole and healed life? Explain.

_____

_____

_____

_____

Read John 5:6. Ask yourself the same question Jesus asks the man: Do you want to be healed? Explain why or why not.

_____

_____

_____

_____

When Jesus encountered a man who was in deep need of healing from wounds that he had carried for thirty-eight years, He asked him if he was serious about getting well (John 5:6). That seems like an odd question that is lacking compassion, but it isn't. No real effort is required in desiring a thing, but acquiring what one desires often requires overcoming a great many obstacles that are in the path of victory. Nothing worth having is ever acquired easily without effort or determination; therefore, if you are a wounded soul who desires healing, I need to ask you if you really want to get well.

I pray that you said yes and that you meant it, because however long or painful your journey of healing may be, the joy of eventually being free is well worth it. At some point, any person with a wounded soul must choose between remaining devastated and being healed and made completely whole.

Do you see yourself as a partner with God in your healing? Explain why or why not.

_____

_____

_____

_____

_____

What part do you think you need to play?

_____

_____

_____

_____

Read the lists of roadblocks in bold. Circle any you have in your life or write other ones on the lines below.

The Roadblock of Avoidance (running away from or ignoring reality, hoping that if you ignore it long enough, your problem will go away)

If you have been running from your past and you desire healing in your soul, let me say to you what God said to me: "It's time!" It is time to learn how to communicate with yourself honestly and stop blaming your past for any current problems that you have. Our past certainly may be the reason we behave in undesirable ways, but we should not let it become an excuse to stay the way we are. Buried feelings have energies of their own. They are alive, and they constantly affect us in adverse ways until we confront and deal with them. No matter how far down we have pushed them into our soul, they will manifest themselves in some way sooner or later. They will not ever simply vanish. They must be dealt with.

The Roadblock of Blame (blaming others for your misery)

The blame game began in the Garden of Eden (Genesis 3) and has never ceased since then. It can be very interesting to begin observing how often we, as well as others, avoid responsibility for our mistakes and behaviors through blaming.

The Roadblock of Excuses (making excuses for your wrong behavior)

I'm sure you have heard the phrase *That is an empty excuse.* And that is exactly what our excuses are. They have no truth in them, and they carry no weight with God. We will find real freedom if we learn to simply say, "I'm sorry, and there is no excuse for my behavior." When we can say that and mean it, it sets us free and goes a long way in helping the people we have hurt to forgive us.

The excuses we can come up with are endless, but they are all simply ways to avoid taking responsibility for our actions, and until we do that, there is no healing.

_____

_____

_____

_____

_____

Explore God's Word

Take time to read the story of Jonah (found in the book of Jonah). Write what happens in your own words.

_____

_____

_____

_____

What can you learn from Jonah's experience and the roadblocks he put up?

_____

_____

_____

_____

Are there any other people in the Bible you can learn from when it comes to dealing with your roadblocks? Explain.

_____

_____

_____

_____

David asked God for mercy and stated that he was conscious of his transgression. He wasn't hiding or running any longer (Psalm 51:1–3). He said that God desires truth in the inner being (Psalm 51:6). Facing truth—whether it is the truth about something that has been done to us or something that we have done to someone else or against God—is the key to the healing of the soul and being set free from the past.

There is nothing we cannot be forgiven for. No amount of sin is too much for God to forgive.

Healing in Action

Write down ways you will overcome the roadblocks that are keeping you from healing.

_____

_____

_____

_____

Now ask God in prayer for specific help to overcome them.

_____

_____

_____

_____

Work together with God for your healing.

Remember

The excuses we can come up with are endless, but they are all simply ways to avoid taking responsibility for our actions, and until we do that, there is no healing.

Create in me a pure heart, O God, and renew a steadfast spirit within me (Psalm 51:10 NIV).

The Roadblock of Self-Pity

Before you begin, read chapter 16 in *Healing the Soul of a Woman*.

In Touch with Yourself

How have you partnered with God to overcome roadblocks to your healing this week? Explain.

_____

_____

_____

_____

Read the opening quote by Martyn Lloyd-Jones. Do you agree or disagree with it? Explain.

_____

_____

_____

_____

Describe a time you have felt sorry for yourself and how self-pity actually made you feel.

_____

_____

_____

_____

Read the story the Cherokee elder told his grandson. What do you think this story means?

_____

_____

_____

_____

Write descriptions or draw a picture of the two wolves. Then circle the one you will feed through your thoughts.

I pray that after reading and meditating on the material in this chapter, you will firmly decide to never waste another hour in self-pity, let alone an entire day, or perhaps even days at a time. The days I wasted feeling sorry for myself are far too many to count. They are days I can never get back, because once a day is gone, we never get to go back and do it over. We can, however, learn from our mistakes and make better choices in the future.

Do you think self-pity has ever helped you? Explain why or why not.

_____

_____

_____

_____

Self-pity comes from an unwillingness to accept a situation or circumstance in your life. It often develops when there are things that we want but cannot have or things we don't want and cannot get rid of. It is a feeling that you are a victim of something or someone. It is fed by meditating over and over on your challenges, difficulties, and problems in life and by comparing your life with someone you think has it better than you do. _Are you feeding the wrong wolf?_

Explore God's Word

Read Peter's words in 1 Peter 1:3. What does it mean to be born into an ever-living hope?

_____

_____

_____

_____

Read Galatians 5:19–23. Write down the works of the flesh, or things we do when we live according to our sinful nature. Look up any word you do not know.

_____

_____

_____

_____

_____

Now note the fruit of the Spirit, the characteristics we display when we are led by God's Spirit.

_____

_____

_____

_____

Healing in Action

List some things you will do when you feel self-pity trying to creep in.

_____

_____

_____

_____

Be proactive! Have a plan of attack before self-pity crops up. Write your plan of action here.

_____

_____

_____

_____

It is time to give up all the excuses and knock the roadblocks in life out of the way so you can move forward. Healing for your soul and an enjoyable life are waiting for you on the other side of the roadblocks. Being free from self-pity, or any of the other roadblocks I have mentioned, certainly may not be the total answer to healing your wounded soul—you may need other help and more time—but it is certainly a great beginning and can only make things better for you. Trust God for total healing, because Jesus can heal you everywhere you hurt!

Remember

Self-pity is a sin, and like any other sin, we need to admit it and repent of it.

But the fruit of the Spirit is love, joy, peace, forbearance, kindness, goodness, faithfulness, gentleness and self-control. Against such things there is no law (Galatians 5:22–23 NIV).

Stand Up for Yourself

Before you begin, read chapter 17 in *Healing the Soul of a Woman*.

In Touch with Yourself

How have you attacked self-pity this week? If so, how did you handle it?

_____

_____

_____

_____

_____

Read the opening quote by Billy Graham. Do you agree or disagree with it? Why?

_____

_____

_____

_____

_____

Reflect on the story of a historical figure who took a stand and changed history. What inspires you in their story?

_____

_____

_____

_____

How can you take a stand today and change your life, regardless of your past?

_____

_____

_____

_____

You might be used to change history for many, but if not, you can at least be someone who changes your own history. Your painful past doesn't ever have to be your destiny—you can take a stand against the wrong behavior of other people who have harmed you, and when you do, you will feel empowered, rather than merely feeling like a helpless victim.

People who are being abused or mistreated need to be courageous, speak up, and take a stand to protect themselves. Most abusive people will back down when confronted. I am familiar with a case in which, for years, the man in the home has been controlling, demeaning, and very quick to get angry when things don't go his way. His wife is meek and tends to be fearful, so she simply put up with his behavior for many years. She has finally started standing up to him, and although they have a long way to go, he is treating her somewhat better. He has been getting counseling regarding his anger issue, and he actually admitted in a counseling session that since she is no longer willing to put up with his bad behavior and is confronting him, he is treating her better.

When you stand up for yourself, how can you make sure you're doing it in the right way and at the right time?

_____

_____

_____

_____

Stand up for yourself, but do it in the right way. Don't become ungodly while trying to deal with the ungodly behavior of others.

Explore God's Word

When a woman has been seriously mistreated, it is unlikely that she has the ability to view things and people in a balanced way as long as she is judging them through her pain. We need God's Word to guide us into what is right, and we need a willing heart that will be obedient to it and view it as the supreme authority in our lives. The only way I learned what right behavior was came through studying God's Word. We don't always want to do what is right, but if what we want to do or feel like doing is not in agreement with God's Word, then we can submit to God's ways, knowing that in the end, they are always right and produce the best result.

How can the Word of God keep you balanced in your behavior?

_____

_____

_____

Which Scriptures have you read throughout this study that can help you personally? List them below. Consider memorizing them.

_____

_____

_____

Read Daniel's account of standing up for what he believed in Daniel 6:7–22. Describe what happened.

_____

_____

_____

How can Daniel's story give you courage?

_____

_____

_____

Healing in Action

Is there something you need to stand up for—or take a step toward—either in your healing or in your life? Explain why you haven't taken a step yet or what is holding you back now.

_____

_____

_____

_____

Pray about the best timing and way to confront the situation. Think of a firm, balanced way to say or do what you need to do. Write your thoughts below.

_____

_____

_____

_____

Remember

Don't let the fear of taking a stand hold you back from being all you can be and doing all that you can do.

Finally, be strong in the Lord and in his mighty power. Put on the full armor of God, so that you can take your stand against the devil's schemes (Ephesians 6:10–11 NIV).

Establish Boundaries—Don't Build Walls

Before you begin, read chapter 18 in *Healing the Soul of a Woman*.

In Touch with Yourself

Describe what happened when you took a stand this week.

_____

_____

_____

Read the opening quote from Henry Cloud. Explain what it means and whether or not you agree with it.

_____

_____

_____

What does it mean to have boundaries in your life? Describe what it looks like.

_____

_____

_____

Evaluate the boundaries in your life. Do you think they protect you, or do you need to draw clearer lines? Explain.

_____

_____

_____

I remember complaining to God about the employer I mentioned who was controlling me, and God surprised me by telling me that I was just as guilty as he was because although he was controlling me, I was letting him do it. Ouch! It is important for us to establish boundaries in all areas of our lives. Some boundaries we set are for ourselves; they may be boundaries for our eating habits, budget, how much we work versus how much we rest, and other things that help us have healthy disciplines in our daily lives. Other boundaries we set are for people. These boundaries prevent us from being hurt, and they help others realize that if they want a relationship with us, they won't be allowed to take advantage of us in the process.

Think about your closest relationships. Are they honest relationships or dishonest relationships? Explain.

_____

_____

_____

_____

_____

The more God works in our lives and heals our wounded souls, the more we enjoy helping other people, and while that is good, we must be careful not to let people take advantage of us. I realized several years ago that I had several one-sided relationships, ones in which I did all the giving and the other party did all of the taking, and I decided that I needed to set some boundaries.

Do you agree with the statement "We truly do not love another person if we let them take advantage of us"? Explain.

_____

_____

_____

_____

_____

Draw or write about what a healthy boundary looks like to you. Think about the difference between setting boundaries and building walls.

_____

_____

_____

Explore God's Word

Read Galatians 6:1–5 from different versions of the Bible. Write down what these verses say to you about how you should treat others.

_____

_____

_____

What other Scriptures can guide you in how to treat others while not letting them take advantage of you?

_____

_____

_____

Some of us choose isolation rather than taking a chance on relationships after we've been hurt, but we cannot make spiritual progress toward becoming like Christ if we do that. For example, we can never learn patience if everything goes our way quickly. We can never learn to love unlovely people or those with habits that annoy us if we are never around them. God uses people with rough edges to sand the rough edges off of us.

How can you view a challenging relationship as a way for you to grow?

_____

_____

_____

Healing in Action

What areas do you need to pray about specifically in regard to establishing healthy boundaries and tearing down walls you've built in your life? How can you continue to grow and be patient with others, but not tolerate unhealthy relationships?

_____

_____

_____

_____

Follow your plan this week and make notes about what happens.

_____

_____

_____

_____

Remember

Dealing with the messiness of relationships can be painful, but in the end, it is worth it.

A friend loves at all times, and kinsfolk are born to share adversity (Proverbs 17:17 NRSV).

Become Your Own Best Ally

Before you begin, read chapter 19 in *Healing the Soul of a Woman*.

In Touch with Yourself

Now that you are more aware of how you should treat others and what you should accept from them, how have your relationships changed?

_____

_____

_____

_____

Read the opening quote from John Maxwell. What do you think it means? Do you agree or disagree with it? Why?

_____

_____

_____

_____

When have you had to deal with rejection or disapproval? Share your thoughts below.

_____

_____

_____

_____

Both Paul and David were used greatly by God, and they encountered many people who were not for them. They were comforted by and comforted others with the knowledge that although we will deal with people who are not for us and do not approve of us, God is always for us, and He is on our side in our times of struggle, pain, and challenge.

It is time that we make a decision to agree with God rather than agreeing with our enemies. Perhaps you have formed an opinion of yourself based on what unkind people have said or thought about you, or how they have treated you. If so, that is a mistake that needs to be corrected. It is time for you to be for you, and that simply means it is time for you to be a friend to yourself, to be your own best ally, and to learn to love yourself in a godly way.

Do you believe the promises of God for your life? Have you come in agreement with God's Word? Explain.

_____

_____

_____

_____

Do you like yourself? Explain.

_____

_____

_____

_____

Do you see and appreciate the talents and abilities that God has given you?

_____

_____

_____

_____

Do you know that you are valuable?

_____

_____

_____

_____

No matter how much God wants to do for and through us, He cannot do any of it unless we come into agreement with Him, and that means we agree with His Word. All of His promises become a reality in our lives only if we believe them. If God says we are greatly loved and filled with His wisdom, then we are. If He says that we are forgiven and that His plan for our future is good, then it is.

What promises of God in His Word have helled you to receive healing for your soul so far?

_____

_____

_____

_____

_____

Explore God's Word

Read David's words in Psalm 118:6. Write what they mean to you.

_____

_____

_____

_____

Reread Psalm 118:6 out loud. Make it a declaration of faith and speak it boldly.

How does this statement of faith encourage you? Do you really believe it's true for you?

_____

_____

_____

_____

_____

Now read Romans 8:31 and answer the question.

_____

_____

_____

_____

How does it help you to know that if God is for you, no one can succeed against you? Does it change your attitude and behavior toward things that need to be confronted in your life?

_____

_____

_____

_____

Learning to like yourself and be your own best ally is one of the best decisions you can ever make. No matter how many people love and admire you, if you don't like yourself, you will never be happy.

Healing in Action

How can the dread of criticism be the death of greatness?

_____

_____

_____

_____

How can the fear of making a wrong decision make you indecisive? Is there any fear in your life that's holding you back?

_____

_____

_____

_____

Trust yourself to be able to follow your heart and to know the best thing that you should do. Never do anything that God's Word doesn't approve of or anything that your conscience tells you is wrong, but always remember that many roads may get you to the same destination, and God has given you the privilege of deciding which road you want to take. The decision you make isn't wrong just because it isn't what someone else would do.

Spend time alone, reflecting on your journey toward the healing of your soul. Focus on the progress you've made so far, not how far you have to go. What will you do to celebrate?

_____

_____

_____

_____

Remember

Be your best friend instead of your worst enemy.

What then are we to say about these things? If God is for us, who is against us? (Romans 8:31 NRSV).

Healing the Wounds of Codependency

Before you begin, read chapter 20 in *Healing the Soul of a Woman*.

In Touch with Yourself

What did you do to celebrate your progress? How did it feel? Plan to take time to celebrate what God is doing in your life moving forward.

_____

_____

_____

_____

Read the opening quote from the unknown author. What does it mean?

_____

_____

_____

_____

Have you ever experienced the pain of watching someone harm themselves through wrong or addictive behavior? What was it like?

_____

_____

_____

_____

Do you, or someone you love, have an addiction problem? How have you tried to deal with it?

_____

_____

_____

_____

Wanting to help someone we love does not mean that we are codependent, but our efforts to help can morph into codependency if we aren't careful. When a person is codependent, it means that their life is controlled by someone else's problems or bad choices. They may never know how any day will go for them because it is dependent on what the troubled person in their life does. I remember numerous times when Dave and I were home and just starting to relax after a challenging day at the office, and I would receive a call letting me know that my brother was in jail or was displaying psychotic behavior and the people he was with didn't know what to do with him. We often had to cancel our plans because of my brother's problems. We should all be willing to change our plans if someone truly needs our help, but if the same person creates the same situation over and over, it is not good.

If you're trying to help someone who doesn't really want to help themselves, you may be putting yourself in an unhealthy situation for you. What changes can you make to correct this?

_____

_____

_____

Do you believe the statement "A mother is never happier than her unhappiest child"? Explain.

_____

_____

_____

_____

Write a prayer now for anyone you know who has an addiction. Journal any thoughts that come to you during your prayer time.

_____

_____

_____

_____

Explore God's Word

Read 1 Peter 5:7. What cares do you need to cast on God?

_____

_____

_____

Draw a picture of yourself casting your cares on God.

How does it feel to release the things you can't control or change?

_____

_____

_____

I recently went through something that was troubling me and stealing my peace, and when I finally faced the real issue behind what was causing my unhappiness, God showed me that I was trying to control what people were doing in a specific situation and I needed to stop. Sometimes I find it difficult to draw the line between being responsible and being controlling, so I continue learning from God in this very important area of life.

How does giving up control of the things you shouldn't take responsibility for help you?

_____

_____

_____

_____

_____

Healing in Action

Review the signs of helping too much. Put a check mark next to any that apply to you.

_____ *Sign 1: You may be helping too much if you resent what you are doing. I believe that when we are doing what God wants us to do, we should feel peace, not resentment.*

_____ *Sign 2: If what you are doing is fostering irresponsibility or incompetence, or if it is making the one you are helping too dependent upon you, it is a sign that you are helping too much.*

_____ *Sign 3: If you have a feeling that you are being manipulated, you are helping too much.*

_____ *Sign 4: If what you intended as a one-time blessing has become a long-term obligation that is now a burden to you, you might be helping too much.*

_____ *Sign 5: If you continue to say yes to the person you are helping when you know in your heart you should say no, you are definitely doing too much.*

_____ *Sign 6: If the person you are helping expects you to do more and more for them instead of being grateful for what you have done, you are helping too much.*

_____ *Sign 7: If you continually cancel your plans because the one you are helping* needs *you to help them, you are probably doing too much for them.*

Write comments about any signs you identify with.

_____

_____

_____

_____

_____

Think about your motives. What is driving you to do what you're doing for others?

_____

_____

_____

_____

_____

It does very little good to ask God to heal our wounded souls if we continue doing things that wound them over and over. God is in the healing business, and He delights in making us whole, but we need to cooperate with Him by doing everything He shows us that we need to do.

What will you do differently now that you have thought about your actions and motives?

_____

_____

_____

_____

_____

Remember

Nothing makes us happier than helping and giving to others when we do it in healthy way and for the right reasons.

Casting the whole of your care [all your anxieties, all your worries, all your concerns, once and for all] on Him, for He cares for you affectionately *and* cares about you watchfully (1 Peter 5:7 AMPC).

CHAPTER 21

The Blessings of a Healthy Soul

Before you begin, read chapter 21 in *Healing the Soul of a Woman*.

In Touch with Yourself

Have you made any changes in relationships that are codependent in your life? If so, how has this affected you personally, as well as the other person in the relationship?

_____

_____

_____

_____

Read Psalm 103:1–3 out loud. Journal your thoughts about what these verses mean to you.

_____

_____

_____

_____

Take some time to revisit what a healthy life and soul looks like to you. How would you describe it?

_____

_____

_____

_____

Illustrate what it looks like to have a healthy soul.

Do you believe that emotional stress drains you of energy? Explain.

_____

_____

_____

_____

_____

I doubt that we can properly ascertain the negative effects that abuse and mental and physical stress have on our health. I was already experiencing problems in my body by the time I was eighteen years old, and it is not surprising, considering the things I had gone through in my life by that time. I can testify that the more peace I have, the better I feel physically. Emotional stress drains us of the energy we need for daily life.

Perhaps you have never realized how much the condition of your soul affects your body, but they are definitely closely connected and affect one another greatly. Therefore, two of the things you can look forward to as you continue your journey of healing are better health and more energy.

Do you believe Jesus is a healer? Explain.

_____

_____

_____

_____

_____

Explore God's Word

Read several verses mentioned in the chapter about health and healing. Write down words that stand out to you or what these Scriptures are saying to you in your own words.

3 John 1:2

_____

_____

Proverbs 17:22

_____

_____

Psalm 41:1-3

_____

_____

_____

Look up an account of Jesus healing someone in the Bible (see Matthew, Mark, Luke and John). After you read the story, journal your thoughts and the things that stood out to you.

_____

_____

_____

Why is confidence a side-effect of a healed soul?

_____

_____

_____

Our confidence should not be in what we can do, but in what Jesus can do through us. Knowing beyond any doubt that we are loved unconditionally gives us courage to do things that we might have otherwise been afraid of. We learn that even when we make mistakes, God still loves us and is ready to help us. Proverbs 24:16 tells us that a righteous man falls seven times and rises again.

We may get knocked down in life, but if we are in Christ and our soul is healthy, we will always get back up again. If you have been lying in your pain and misery, watching from the sidelines as your life goes by, it is time for you to get up and get going again.

Healing in Action

Read the findings from the self-esteem study commissioned by Dove. Which statistics surprise you? Which do not? Explain.

_____

_____

_____

_____

It is sad when girls and women spend their lives trying to find confidence in how they look, because no matter how good we look, there will always be someone who may look better according to the world's standards. Our confidence and beauty can be found in knowing Christ and becoming like Him.

Do you need to find confidence in Christ, rather than in how you look? Explain.

_____

_____

_____

_____

How are your family and friends impacted by the healing of your soul?

_____

_____

_____

_____

_____

Relationships are a large part of life, and we all want to enjoy good ones. Doing so becomes very difficult if we live with wounds, bruises, and pain in our inner life. We don't mean to hurt people, but we do. Because what is in us is what comes out of us.

I am glad that I pressed through not only for myself but also for my family, friends, and all the people I touch in my daily life. Everywhere we go, we are affecting and touching people. At home, at school, at work, at church, or in our neighborhoods, we leave an impression on people. Whether I smile or don't smile at someone leaves an impression on them concerning what they think of me. If I am discouraged and depressed because of my pain and unhappiness, I am more likely not to smile or be friendly than if I am healed and happy. An act as simple as smiling at others can make them feel better about themselves. Our contact with others may be brief, but in some ways it may be lasting. People may not remember what we said to them, but they remember how we made them feel. The better you feel about yourself, the better you will make others feel about themselves.

What benefits of a healthy soul are you looking forward to?

_____

_____

_____

_____

_____

Remember all of the benefits you can as you keep pressing toward a healthy soul.

Remember

The better you feel about yourself, the better you will make others feel about themselves.

> I press on toward the goal to win the prize for which God has called me heavenward in Christ Jesus (Philippians 3:14 NIV).

The Painless Path

Before you begin, read chapter 22 in *Healing the Soul of a Woman*.

In Touch with Yourself

Which benefits of a healthy soul have you focused on this week? How has remembering these benefits helped you continue to press toward your goal or complete restoration?

_____

_____

_____

_____

Read the opening quote by the unknown author. What do you think it means in regard to the healing of your soul?

_____

_____

_____

_____

Do you want a painless path? Explain.

_____

_____

_____

_____

Our flesh always looks for the easy way out, but I don't want to give you false hope, so I will say openly that if your soul has been severely wounded through abuse, rejection, loss, abandonment, long-term illness, or any other thing, the journey toward healing won't be painless. But once you are healed, you can keep and enjoy it for the rest of your life.

What kind of fleshly baggage are you still carrying on this journey? Explain.

_____

_____

_____

We are triune beings: we are a spirit, we have a soul, and we live in a body. When the Bible refers to "the flesh," it is speaking of the body and soul (mind, will, and emotions) combined. The flesh is very different from the spirit. When we are born again (receive Christ through faith), Jesus comes to live in us and our spirit is filled with His Spirit, who seeks to guide us through life. God wants us to choose what is right, but He never forces us to do it.

Paul urged believers to "walk" in the spirit and not in the flesh. The spirit is holy and good, but the flesh is filled with tendencies toward evil. If, for example, a believer is walking in (or according to) the flesh and someone offends her, she will follow her feelings and choose to be angry and resentful, carrying a grudge and perhaps seeking revenge. On the other hand, if a believer is walking in (or according to) the Spirit, she will resist the temptation to be touchy and will choose to quickly forgive. She doesn't necessarily make this choice because it is the easy one or the one she thinks is fair or feels like doing, but she chooses it because it is the will of God. This is what it means to walk in the Spirit and not in the flesh.

Do you think you spend more time walking in the flesh or walking in the Spirit? Explain.

_____

_____

_____

Have you been able to discern when the Spirit is leading you one way or another? Explain.

_____

_____

_____

_____

Explore God's Word

How would you describe your journey toward healing in terms of fast versus slow, the narrow path versus the wide path?

_____

_____

_____

_____

What ways can you encourage yourself to stay on the path?

_____

_____

_____

_____

What Scriptures remind you to stay the course?

_____

_____

_____

_____

Diamonds are among some of the most valued jewels on earth, and they are formed very slowly, at high temperatures under great pressure from being buried in the depths of the earth.

Geodes are rocks that have an ugly exterior but are magnificently beautiful on the inside because the inner lining is coated with crystals of various colors.

We can use the examples of diamonds and geodes as we think about ourselves. As we begin our journey with God toward healing and wholeness, our behavior may be quite unattractive, but inside of us (in our spirit), where the Holy Spirit lives, there is great beauty and capacity for good. It takes time for us to go through the transformation process so that the work God has done on the inside of us is revealed in our outer lives. And we will experience heat and pressure in the journey to break off the outer hull so what is inside can be poured out. But when the work is done, we are in awe of the magnificent change God has created in us.

Draw a picture of a diamond or something else that will remind you of the way God creates beauty in our lives through the pain we experience.

Healing in Action

Are you ready to accept the pain of continuing the healing process? Explain what you will do to keep yourself on track, moving forward, when the pain seems unbearable.

_____

_____

_____

_____

_____

Most of us would prefer life without any pain, but when it comes to making a choice to let God heal our wounds or stay the way we are, we have to pick our pain. Do you want the temporary pain of progress or the eternal pain of staying the same?

Compare your temporary pain of healing to the eternal pain of staying the same.

_____

_____

_____

_____

Determine today that by God's grace, you will choose the temporary pain that produces healing and trust Him to bring you through the process to total restoration!

Remember

You have a great victory waiting for you, and each step you take in the right direction brings you a little closer to it.

> …We also glory in our sufferings, because we know that suffering produces perseverance; perseverance, character; and character, hope (Romans 5:3–4 NIV).

CHAPTER 23

The Great Exchange

Before you begin, read chapter 23 in *Healing the Soul of a Woman.*

In Touch with Yourself

How has comparing the pain of change to the pain of staying the same helped you press on toward healing?

_____

_____

_____

Read the opening Scripture from Isaiah 6:1–3. What do you think it means in regard to the healing of your soul?

_____

_____

_____

Picture Jesus inviting you to exchange the bad, destructive things in your life for the new, life-giving blessings He offers you. What do you need to exchange?

_____

_____

_____

If we are willing to give ourselves—everything we are and have—to Jesus, He will give us everything He has and is (John 16:15). What He offers is immeasurably better than what we give up. Just think of it: Everything the Father has is ours, and all we need to do is give up our old ideas and ways in order to experience it in every area of our lives.

Why do you think it is tough to let go of the old and familiar?

_____

_____

_____

Is it difficult for you to let go of something you know you need to give to Jesus? If so, share what it is and why.

_____

_____

_____

Explore God's Word

Read each Scripture from several versions of the Bible and write how each verse applies to you and your healing.

_____

_____

_____

John 16:15

_____

_____

_____

Isaiah 61:1-3

_____

_____

_____

Romans 8:28

_____

_____

_____

2 Corinthians 5:17

_____

_____

_____

2 Corinthians 5:21

_____

_____

_____

Jesus has opened the prison doors, and all we need to do is walk out and start our new life with Him. He came to set captives free and to help those who have been afflicted and are brokenhearted. He not only opens the prison doors, according to Isaiah, but He opens our eyes. Even if the doors to the prison we live in have been opened, we won't walk out unless we see that they are open, and God's Word shows us that they are. It makes me very sad when I think about how many believers in Christ live with wounded souls because they have not been told that Jesus has opened the prison doors and they can be free.

Jesus wants to comfort those who mourn, who are sad and grieving. He came to announce the good news that now is the time for God's favor. Perhaps you have always felt like the tail end of everything in life. Perhaps you were the one who was never picked to be on the team or who never received an award when they were being given out. You may have felt last in your life, but it is a new day—the day of the favor of God!

Healing in Action

Jesus is called "the Lamb of God, Who takes away the sin of the world" (John 1:29). When John made that announcement, the Jews knew what he meant because they often used a lamb for their sacrifices. Jesus offers us the great exchange—He takes our sin and we receive His forgiveness. Under the Old Covenant sin was covered, but Jesus removes our sin as far as the east is from the west.

Write a psalm, praise song or letter thanking God for providing the great exchange. Receive His love, mercy, and everything else He desires to give you.

_____

_____

_____

The list of things we can exchange is far too long for me to share all of them in this book, but there is another book that contains them all: the Bible. I want to encourage you to read and study it so you can discover everything God has for you—not as a religious obligation or because you feel it is your duty as a Christian. The Bible is simply the greatest book on the earth, and it is filled with promises that are astounding…and they are all yours in Christ!

Remember

God helps us, answers our prayers, provides for us, and loves us unconditionally, and we don't deserve any of it. But because of His great mercy, it is ours as a gift from Him.

> Let us then approach God's throne of grace with confidence, so that we may receive mercy and find grace to help us in our time of need (Hebrews 4:16 NIV).

WHO YOU ARE IN CHRIST JESUS

Use appendix II in *Healing the Soul of a Woman* or the Bible reference to complete the verses. When you are done, write your own declaration or statement of faith (based on these verses as well as others you have learned during this journey) to describe who you are in Christ. Post your statement and repeat it often.

I have received the spirit of wisdom and revelation in the knowledge of Jesus, the eyes of my understanding being _____ (Ephesians 1:17–18).

I have received the power of the Holy Spirit to lay hands on the sick and see them recover, to cast out demons, to speak with new tongues. I have power over all the power of the enemy, and nothing shall by any means _____ me (Mark 16:17–18; Luke 10:17–19).

I have put off the old man and have put on the _____ man, which is renewed in the knowledge after the image of Him who created me (Colossians 3:9–10).

I have given, and it is _____ to me; good measure, pressed down, shaken together, and running over, men give into my bosom (Luke 6:38).

I have no _____ for my God supplies all of my need according to His riches in glory by Christ Jesus (Philippians 4:19).

I can quench all the fiery darts of the wicked one with my shield of
_____ (Ephesians 6:16).

I can do all things through _____ _____ (Philippians 4:13).

I show forth the praises of God Who has called me out of darkness into
His marvelous _____ (1 Peter 2:9).

I am God's _____, for I am born again of the incorruptible
seed of the Word of God, which lives and abides forever (1 Peter 1:23).

I am God's _____, created in Christ unto good works (Ephesians 2:10).

I am a _____ creature in Christ (2 Corinthians 5:17).

I am a spirit being _____ to God (Romans 6:11; Thessalonians 5:23).

I am a believer, and the _____ of the Gospel shines in my
mind (2 Corinthians 4:4).

I am a _____ of the Word and blessed in my actions (James
1:22, 25).

I am a _____ _____ with Christ (Romans 8:17).

I am more than a _____ through Him Who loves me
(Romans 8:37).

I am an overcomer by the blood of the Lamb and the word of my
_____ (Revelation 12:11).

I am a _____ of His divine nature (2 Peter 1:3–4).

I am an _____ for Christ (2 Corinthians 5:20).

I am part of a _____ generation, a royal priesthood, a holy nation, a purchased people (1 Peter 2:9).

I am the _____ of God in Jesus Christ (2 Corinthians 5:21).

I am the _____ of the Holy Spirit; I am not my own (1 Corinthians 6.19).

I am the _____ and not the tail; I am above only and not beneath (Deuteronomy 28:13).

I am the _____ of the world (Matthew 5:14).

I am His _____, full of mercy, kindness, humility, and long suffering (Romans 8:33; Colossians 3:12).

I am _____ of all my sins and washed in the Blood (Ephesians 1:7).

I am delivered from the power of _____ and translated into God's kingdom (Colossians 1:13).

I am _____ from the curse of sin, sickness, and poverty (Deuteronomy 28:15–68; Galatians 3:13).

I am firmly rooted, built up, established in my faith, and overflowing with _____ (Colossians 2:7).

I am called of God to be the _____ of His praise (Psalm 66:8; 2 Timothy 1:9).

I am healed by the stripes of _____ (Isaiah 53:5; 1 Peter 2:24).

I am _____ _____ with Christ and seated in heavenly places (Ephesians 2:6; Colossians 2:12).

I am greatly loved by _____ (Romans 1:7; Ephesians 2:4; Colossians 3:12; 1 Thessalonians 1:4).

I am strengthened with all might according to His glorious _____ (Colossians 1:11).

I am

Do you have a real relationship with Jesus?

God loves you! He created you to be a special, unique, one-of-a-kind individual, and He has a specific purpose and plan for your life. And through a personal relationship with your Creator—God—you can discover a way of life that will truly satisfy your soul.

No matter who you are, what you've done, or where you are in your life right now, God's love and grace are greater than your sin—your mistakes. Jesus willingly gave His life so you can receive forgiveness from God and have new life in Him. He's just waiting for you to invite Him to be your Savior and Lord.

If you are ready to commit your life to Jesus and follow Him, all you have to do is ask Him to forgive your sins and give you a fresh start in the life you are meant to live. Begin by praying this prayer...

> *Lord Jesus, thank You for giving Your life for me and forgiving me of my sins so I can have a personal relationship with You. I am sincerely sorry for the mistakes I've made, and I know I need You to help me live right.*

> *Your Word says in Romans 10:9, "If you declare with your mouth, 'Jesus is Lord,' and believe in your heart that God raised him from the dead, you will be saved" (NIV). I believe You are the Son of God and confess You as my Savior and Lord. Take me just as I am, and work in my heart, making me the person You want me to be. I want to live for You, Jesus, and I am so grateful that You are giving me a fresh start in my new life with You today.*

> *I love You, Jesus!*

It's so amazing to know that God loves us so much! He wants to have a deep, intimate relationship with us that grows every day as we spend time with Him in prayer and Bible study. And we want to encourage you in your new life in Christ.

Please visit joycemeyer.org/salvation to request Joyce's book *A New Way of Living*, which is our gift to you. We also have other free resources online to help you make progress in pursuing everything God has for you.

Congratulations on your fresh start in your life in Christ! We hope to hear from you soon.

ABOUT THE AUTHOR

JOYCE MEYER is one of the world's leading practical Bible teachers. A *New York Times* bestselling author, Joyce's books have helped millions of people find hope and restoration through Jesus Christ. Joyce's programs, *Enjoying Everyday Life* and *Everyday Answers with Joyce Meyer*, air around the world on television, radio, and the Internet. Through Joyce Meyer Ministries, Joyce teaches internationally on a number of topics with a particular focus on how the Word of God applies to our everyday lives. Her candid communication style allows her to share openly and practically about her experiences so others can apply what she has learned to their lives.

Joyce has authored more than one hundred books, which have been translated into more than one hundred languages, and over 65 million of her books have been distributed worldwide. Bestsellers include *Power Thoughts*; *The Confident Woman*; *Look Great, Feel Great*; *Starting Your Day Right*; *Ending Your Day Right*; *Approval Addiction*; *How to Hear from God*; *Beauty for Ashes*; and *Battlefield of the Mind*.

Joyce's passion to help hurting people is foundational to the vision of Hand of Hope, the missions arm of Joyce Meyer Ministries. Hand of Hope provides worldwide humanitarian outreaches such as feeding programs, medical care, orphanages, disaster response, human trafficking intervention and rehabilitation, and much more—always sharing the love and gospel of Christ.

JOYCE MEYER MINISTRIES

U.S. AND FOREIGN OFFICE
ADDRESSES

Joyce Meyer Ministries
P.O. Box 655
Fenton, MO 63026
USA
(636) 349-0303

Joyce Meyer Ministries—Canada
P.O. Box 7700
Vancouver, BC V6B 4E2
Canada
(800) 868-1002

Joyce Meyer Ministries—Australia
Locked Bag 77
Mansfield Delivery Centre
Queensland 4122
Australia
(07) 3349 1200

Joyce Meyer Ministries—England
P.O. Box 1549
Windsor SL4 1GT
United Kingdom
01753 831102

Joyce Meyer Ministries—South Africa
P.O. Box 5
Cape Town 8000
South Africa
(27) 21-701-1056

OTHER BOOKS BY JOYCE MEYER

JOYCE MEYER SPANISH TITLES

20 Maneras de hacer que cada día sea major (20 Ways to Make Every Day Better)

Aproveche su día (Seize the Day)

Belleza en Lugar de Cenizas (Beauty for Ashes)

Buena Salud, Buena Vida (Good Health, Good Life)

Cambia Tus Palabras, Cambia Tu Vida (Change Your Words, Change Your Life)

El Campo de Batalla de la Mente (Battlefield of the Mind)

Como Formar Buenos Habitos y Romper Malos Habitos (Making Good Habits, Breaking Bad Habits)

Confianza inquebrantable (Unshakeable Trust)

La Conexión de la Mente (The Mind Connection)

Dios No Está Enojado Contigo (God Is Not Mad at You)

La Dosis de Aprobación (The Approval Fix)

Empezando Tu Día Bien (Starting Your Day Right)

Hazte Un Favor a Ti Mismo…Perdona (Do Yourself a Favor…Forgive)

Madre Segura de sí Misma (The Confident Mom)

Pensamientos de Poder (Power Thoughts)

Sobrecarga (Overload) *

Termina Bien tu Día (Ending Your Day Right)

Usted Puede Comenzar de Nuevo (You Can Begin Again)

Viva amando su vida (Living a Life You Love)

Viva Valientemente (Living Courageously)

* Study guide available for this title

BOOKS BY DAVE MEYER

Life Lines